Marie-Josée Thibault

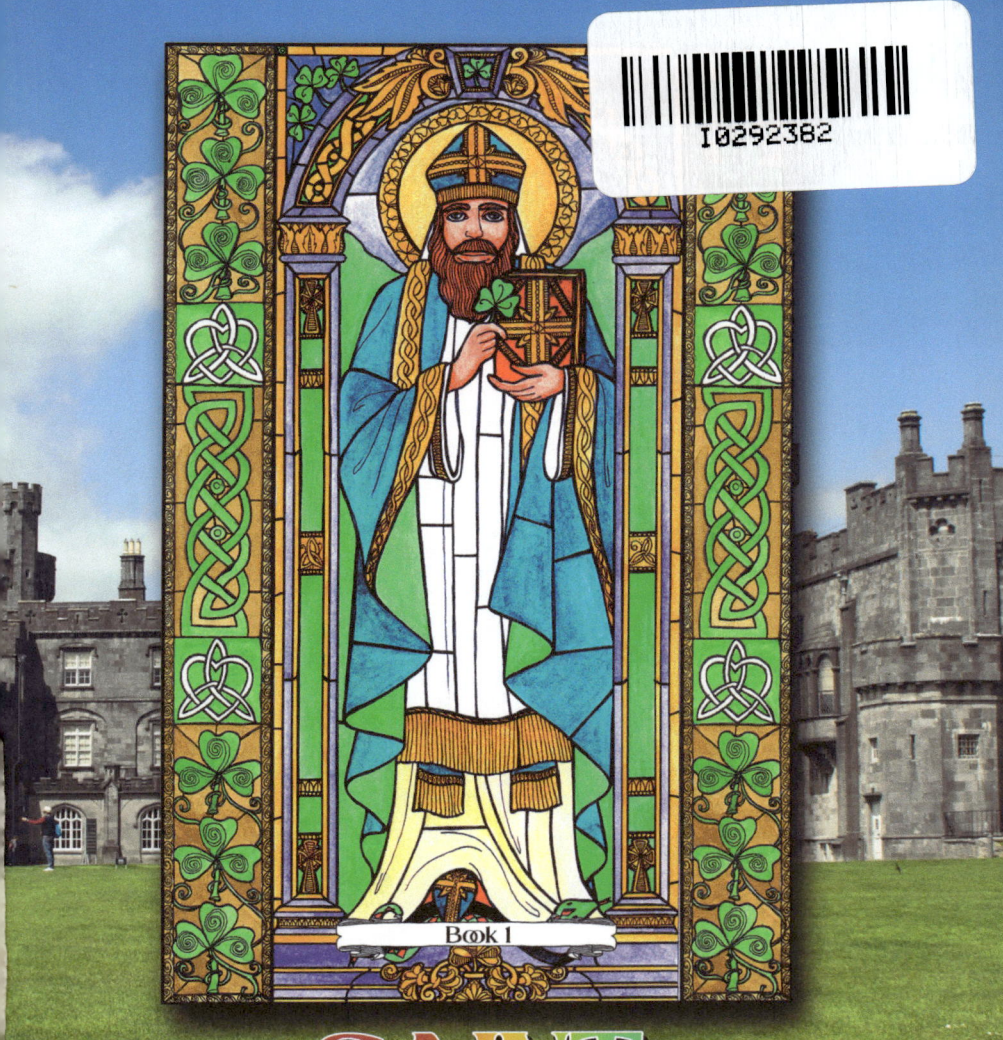

Book 1

SAINT
PATRICK
SPEAKS

Saint Patrick Speaks - Book 1

Published by Abba Books LLC
abbabooksllc@gmail.com

Copyright © 2025 Marie-Josée Thibault

All Rights Reserved

No part of this publication may be reproduced, distributed, or transmitted in any form or by any means, including photocopying, recording, or other electronic or mechanical methods, without the prior written permission of the publisher.

First Edition, 2025
Designed and Edited by Abba Books LLC
ISBN: 978-1-967429-05-9

Abba Books LLC
34972 Newark Blvd, #441
Newark, CA 94560

www.abbamyfatheriloveyou.com
https://www.facebook.com/AbbaILoveYouBooks/

Thy Peace on Earth must be achieved. No light, no litany must be spared to honor Thy Grace.
-Saint Paul

TABLE OF CONTENT

					Chap 17 — 39	
					Chap 18 — 41	
		Chap 8 — 17			Chap 19 — 43	
Preface — VI		Chap 9 — 19			Chap 20 — 47	
Chap 1 — 1		Chap 10 — 21			Chap 21 — 51	
Chap 2 — 3		Chap 11 — 25			Chap 22 — 53	
Chap 3 — 5		Chap 12 — 27			Chap 23 — 55	
Chap 4 — 7		Chap 13 — 29			Chap 24 — 57	
Chap 5 — 9		Chap 14 — 31			Chap 25 — 59	
Chap 6 — 13		Chap 15 — 33			Chap 26 — 61	
Chap 7 — 15		Chap 16 — 37			Chap 27 — 63	

PREFACE

My children of this distressed Earth, listen to me carefully.

Saint Patrick is a logos of universal and divine teaching sourced from the Heart of Abba Father. This teaching is in continuity with the geographical and historical Ireland you know and the unique Spiritual Heritage it contains.

Saint Patrick fulfilled his mission to perfection, and the blessing bestowed by his grace onto Ireland is unique, powerful, universal, and—above all—rooted in love.

I bless you, and I love you.

Saint John Paul II

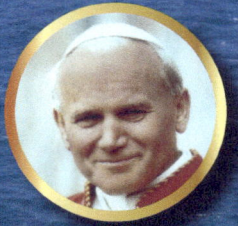

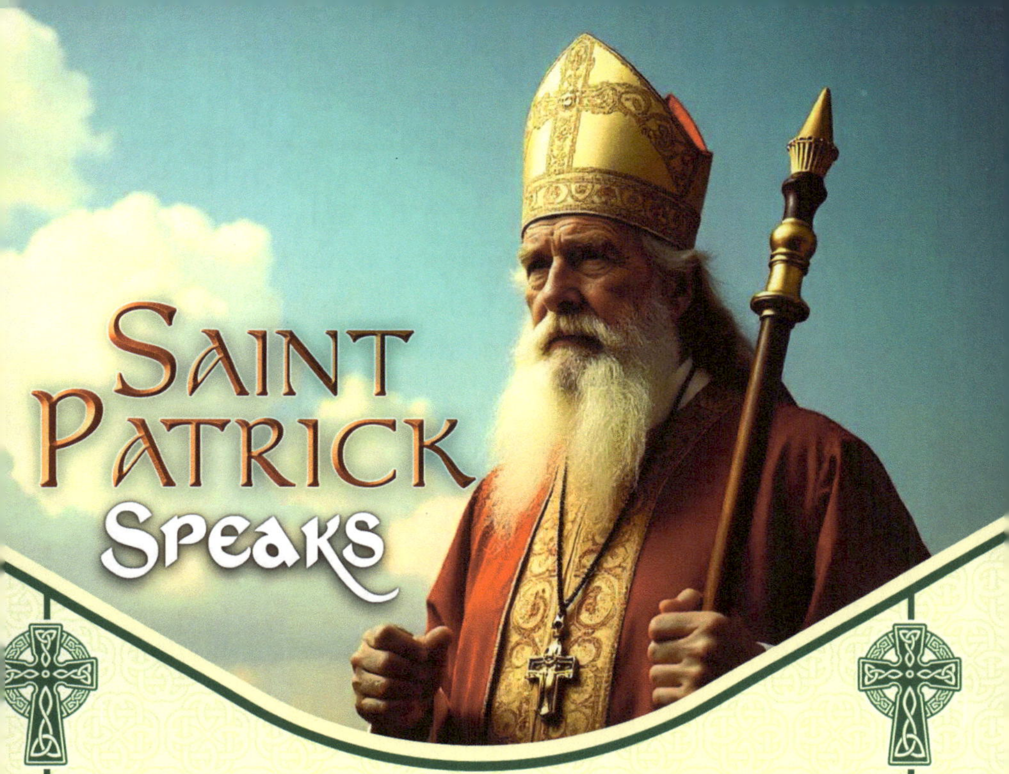

Saint Patrick Speaks

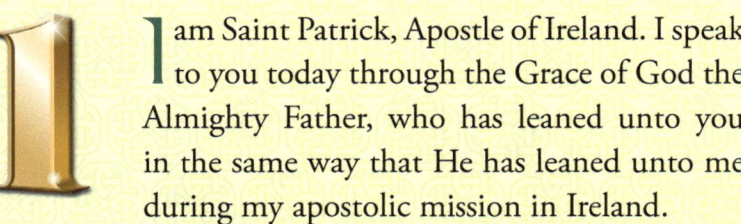

1 I am Saint Patrick, Apostle of Ireland. I speak to you today through the Grace of God the Almighty Father, who has leaned unto you in the same way that He has leaned unto me during my apostolic mission in Ireland.

I give thanks to Him in your name and in mine for these great miracles, which bear witness to the goodness and love of God for all His children in all ages of humanity, for I am Saint Patrick, Apostle of Ireland, and my life in Heaven is dedicated to your evangelization and your conversion to Christ, wherever you are on Earth, whether you are in Ireland or not.

Verily, verily I say unto you: The Father has granted Mercy to my soul thirsting for Him, and He has given me the apostolic gift of teaching the Spiritual Heritage to all the souls on Earth and throughout the ages.

Consequently, I have continuously influenced your life since my death, although you did not know it.

Through the intermediary of the Holy Spirit, who operates this communication today in Marie-Josée, the essence of Saint Paul on Earth, I rejoice that my voice is heard once again on Earth.

I bless you in the Name of the Father, of the Son and of the Holy Spirit and I love you.

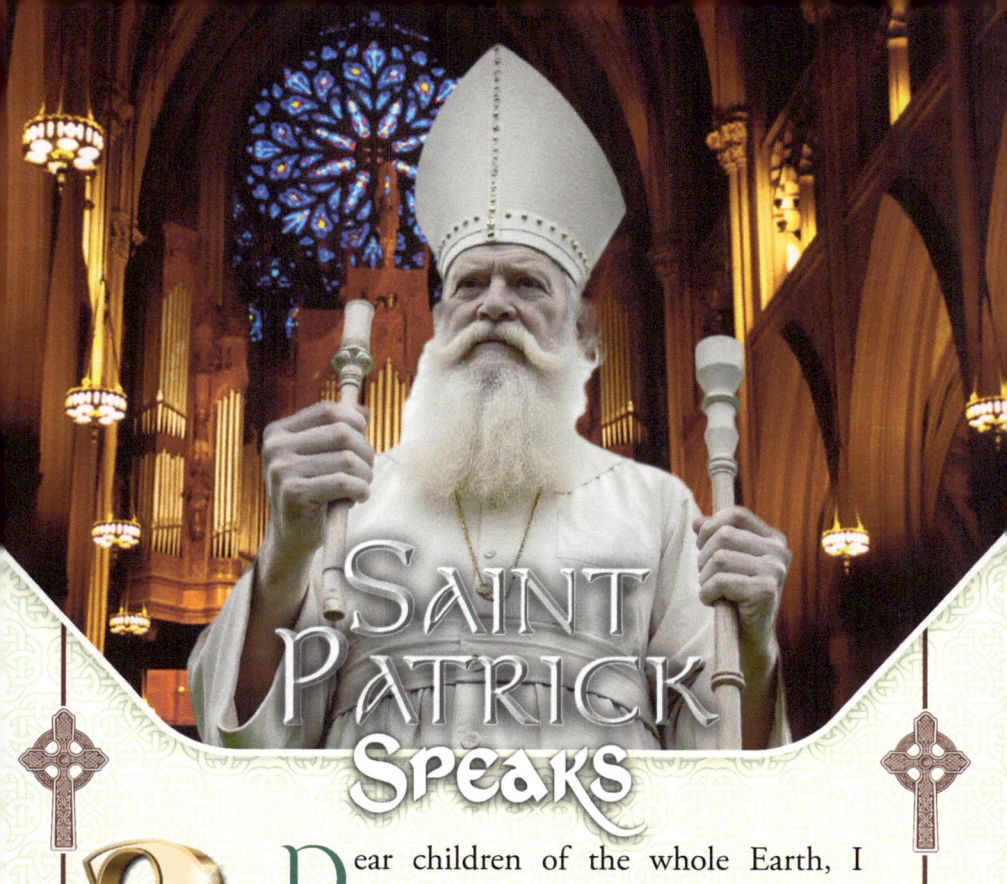

Saint Patrick Speaks

2

Dear children of the whole Earth, I cannot contain my pleasure and wonder at being able to speak to you now. I thank Marie-Josée, the one taking this dictation at this time, and I keep her very close to me and place her under my divine protection.

Ireland has changed enormously, and all of Earth has changed tremendously, but the hearts of men do not change. Righteousness is the same as it was in the past, and falsehood and darkness are the same too. Oh! What sadness overcomes me when I see so much stupidity, so much vanity, so much materialism, all of which defile the soul and the body! Wake up! For the end times are here, dear children of my divine heart. It is with great sorrow that I announce that horrible times are quickly approaching you.

But do not fear, dear friends of my heart of love, I will protect you. I will show you the way toward the perfection of your soul in the eyes of God, for what is important is that God is pleased with you.

I love you.

Saint Patrick Speaks

3 My friends from all over the world, my Irish children scattered across the surface of the globe, listen to me carefully.

The Earth is in a great peril that is much more serious than you can imagine. The Father has decided that a Great Day of Purification is necessary to eliminate the evil that has infiltrated the entire Earth and is ravaging souls and bodies.

I say unto you, I say unto you verily: The end times are fast approaching, and there is very little time left to do to prepare your soul for the Judgment of God, which is very near.

As a result of my tasks as an apostle and evangelizer in Ireland, my mission today is to make your soul perfect in the eyes of God.

The end times are near—I repeat this unto you. Human assistance will be of no help to you when night falls.

I love you.

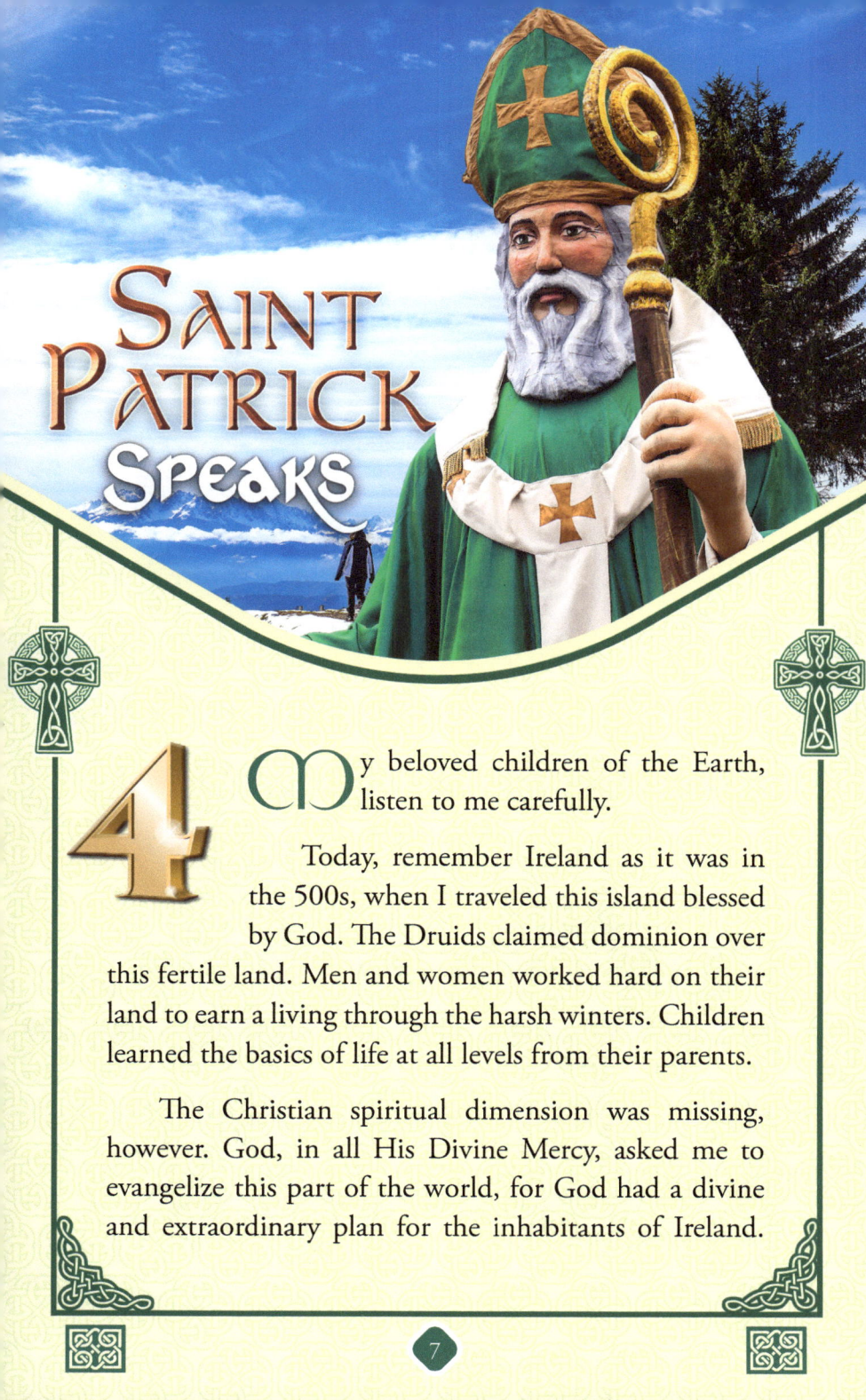

Saint Patrick Speaks

My beloved children of the Earth, listen to me carefully.

Today, remember Ireland as it was in the 500s, when I traveled this island blessed by God. The Druids claimed dominion over this fertile land. Men and women worked hard on their land to earn a living through the harsh winters. Children learned the basics of life at all levels from their parents.

The Christian spiritual dimension was missing, however. God, in all His Divine Mercy, asked me to evangelize this part of the world, for God had a divine and extraordinary plan for the inhabitants of Ireland.

For the proof, look at the countless numbers of deeply Catholic Irish people who populated and converted not only Ireland but the rest of the world. The Catholic faith has taken deep roots in the hearts of the Irish, and this faith has borne much fruit throughout the world. In this, and in many other things, the Father rejoices.

Now in Paradise, I thank God from the depths of my heart for having supported me and for having guided me with so much love, so much wisdom, when I was His apostle on Earth. Christ is with you.

I love you.

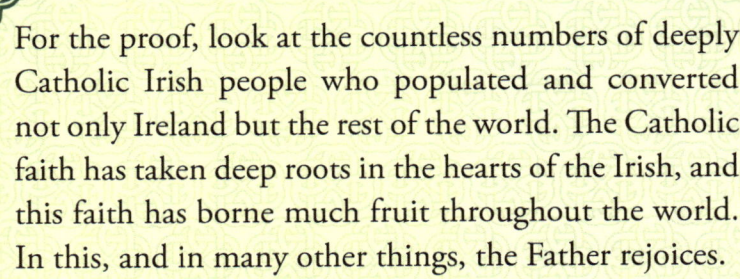

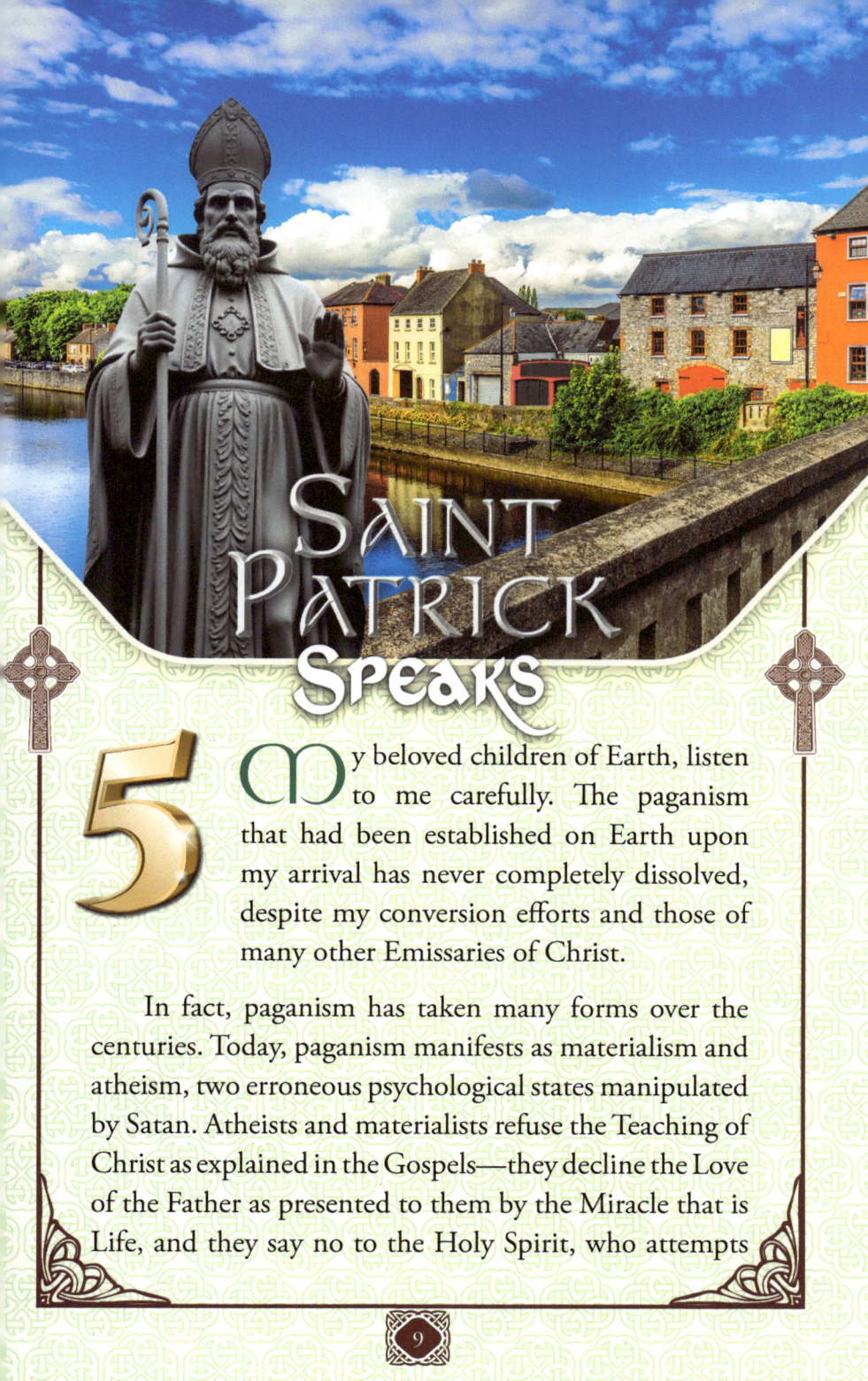

Saint Patrick Speaks

5

My beloved children of Earth, listen to me carefully. The paganism that had been established on Earth upon my arrival has never completely dissolved, despite my conversion efforts and those of many other Emissaries of Christ.

In fact, paganism has taken many forms over the centuries. Today, paganism manifests as materialism and atheism, two erroneous psychological states manipulated by Satan. Atheists and materialists refuse the Teaching of Christ as explained in the Gospels—they decline the Love of the Father as presented to them by the Miracle that is Life, and they say no to the Holy Spirit, who attempts

I love you more than the words written on this page can express.

~ Saint Patrick

to guide them towards numerous opportunities for conversion and transformation in their hearts.

I say unto you, I say unto you verily: materialists and atheists will be subject to the Judgment of God very soon, for God has decided so. Christ is in you.

I love you.

Saint Patrick Speaks

My beloved children of the Earth in peril, listen to me carefully. Today, more than any other day in your life, I want you to focus on your beating heart.

Who gave you the Fire of Life? Who will take it away? Who directs the impulses of the soul that unfold in your heart? Who is responsible for the lasting and true Peace that takes place when you are in a state of prayer or mystical concentration?

I say unto you, I say unto you verily, your heart is the seat of the soul and your soul dwells both on Earth and in Heaven with us. This is why we, the Saints in Paradise, can communicate with you, assist you on your path toward God, support you when your faith falters.

Above all, our Divine and Personal Faith teaches you in a unique and particular way as part of the Teaching of Christ, for our mission on Earth and in Heaven is always the same.

Therefore, I will teach you the Apostolic Faith in God, through Christ my King, as I did among the Nation of Ireland 1,500 years ago. Christ is in you.

I love you.

Saint Patrick Speaks

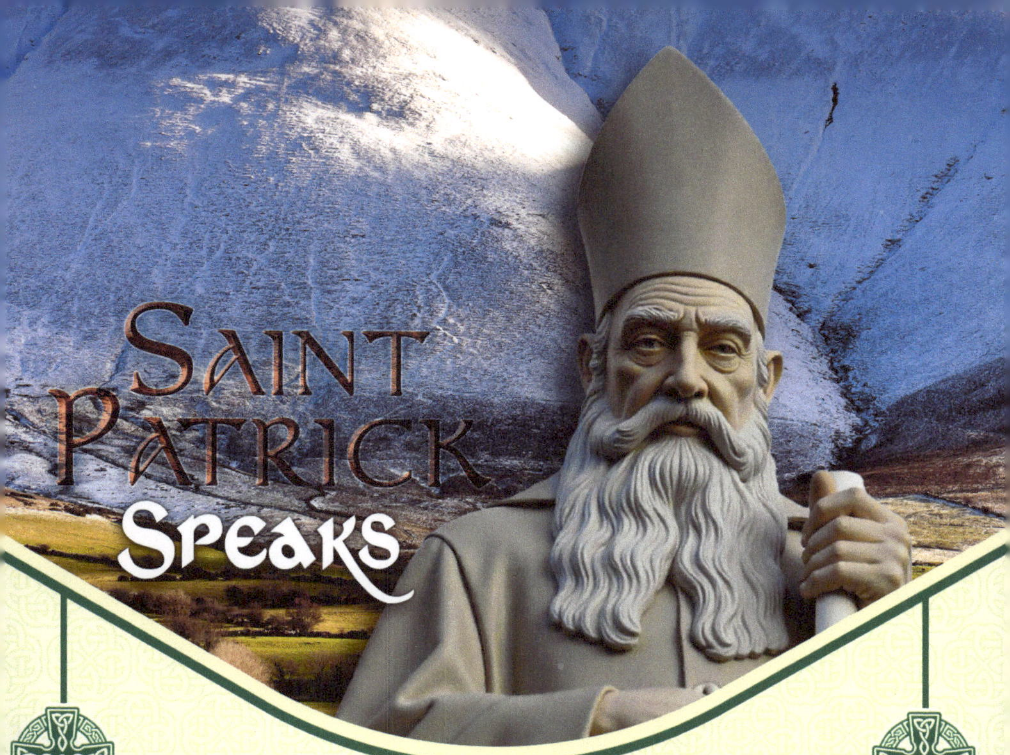

7 My children, my beloveds of Divine Love, listen to me carefully. God shows Mercy upon your soul, dear heart, by giving me the opportunity to speak to you and teach you, thanks to the work of the Logos of Saint Paul on Earth.

I thank Marie-Josée, my friend in the Good News, who hears my words today and who transmits them to you fully and authentically. Marie-Josée is the essence of Saint Paul on Earth, and her apostolic mission is unique and difficult in the same way that my mission on Earth was unique and difficult—we both follow the example of Christ, our Lord and our God.

Read this book and all the books in this collection carefully, for Saint Paul Himself is at work here. Christ is in you.

I love you.

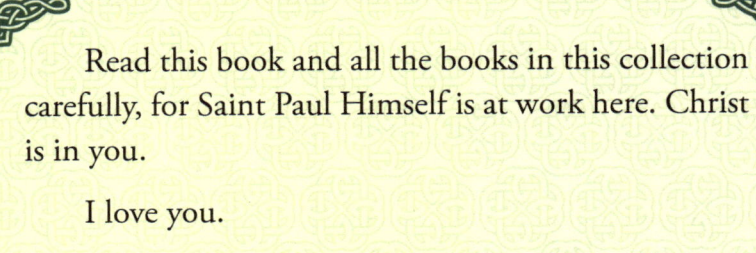

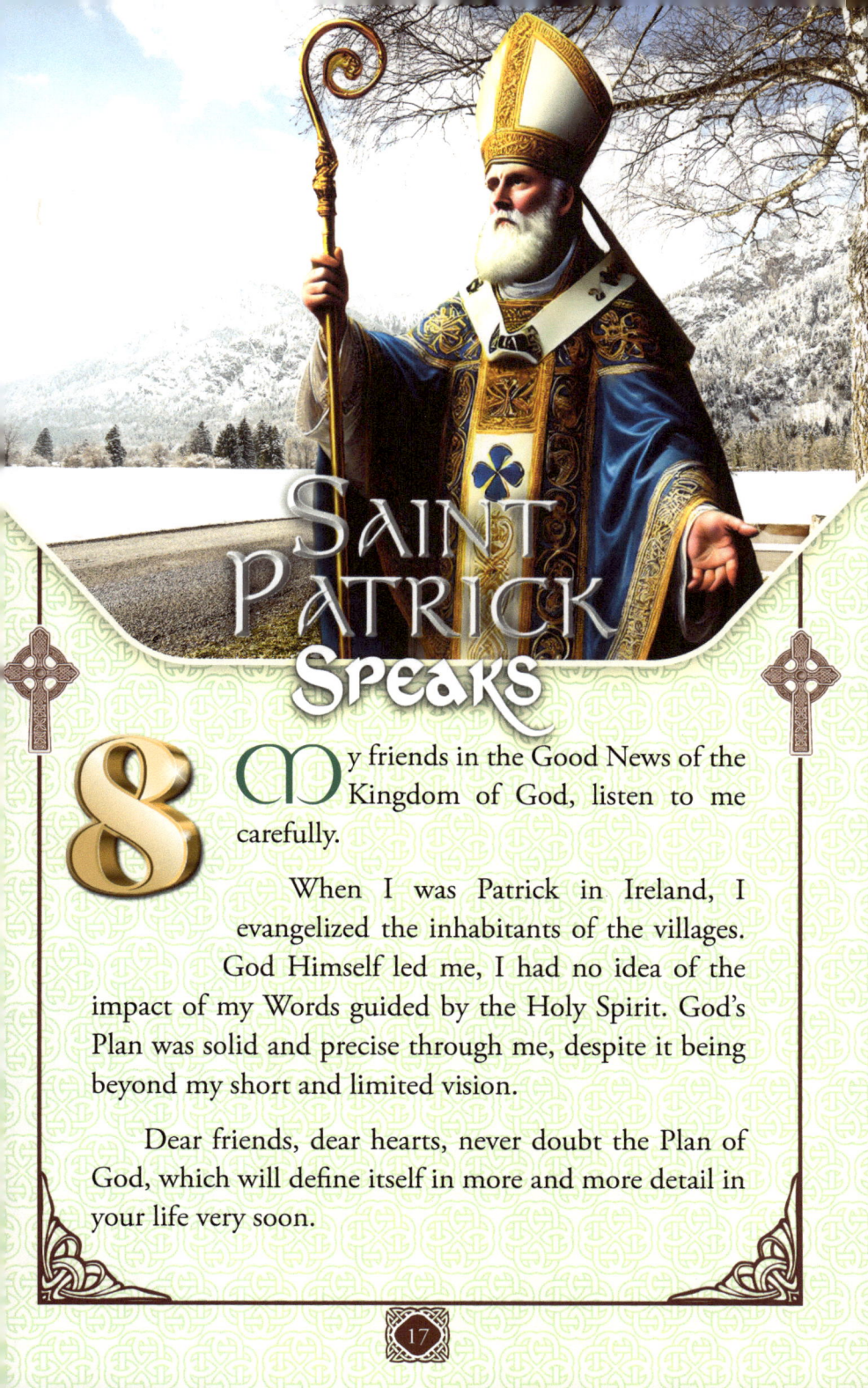

Saint Patrick Speaks

8

My friends in the Good News of the Kingdom of God, listen to me carefully.

When I was Patrick in Ireland, I evangelized the inhabitants of the villages. God Himself led me, I had no idea of the impact of my Words guided by the Holy Spirit. God's Plan was solid and precise through me, despite it being beyond my short and limited vision.

Dear friends, dear hearts, never doubt the Plan of God, which will define itself in more and more detail in your life very soon.

For God also has a mission for you, dear readers! Oh, yes! I hasten to add that I, Saint Patrick of Ireland, the Saint of Spiritual Heritage, will personally participate in this mission and assist you every day of your life as you carry out your mission to perfection. Christ is in you.

I love you.

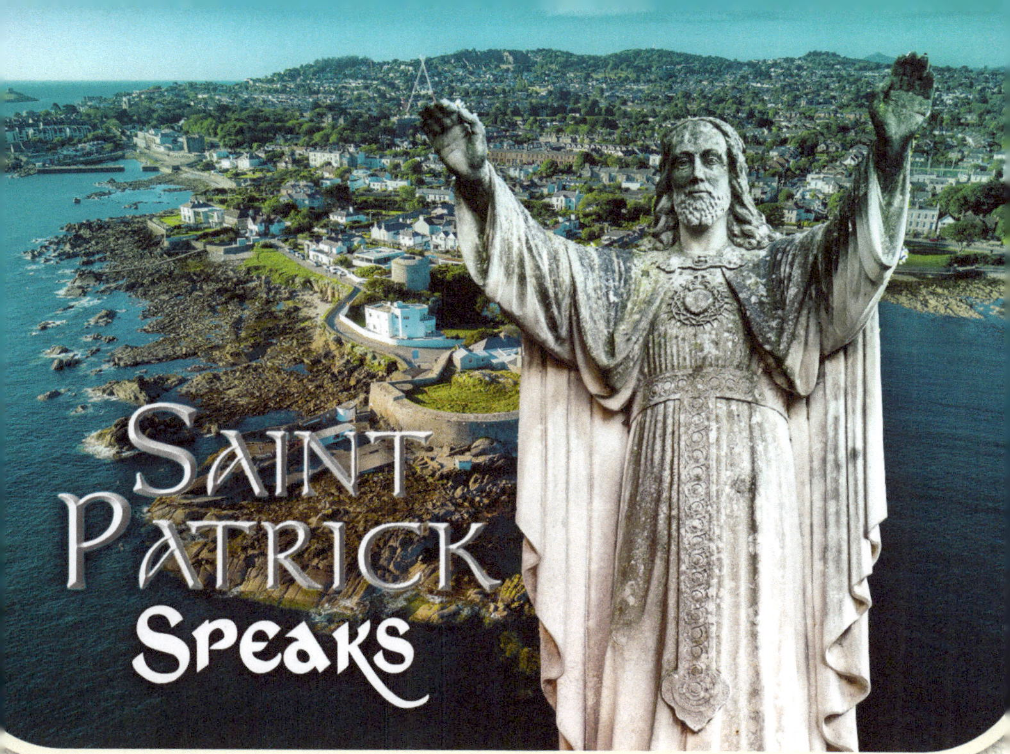

Saint Patrick Speaks

9 My friends, my children, my little ones of Earth, listen to me carefully.

Christ is in you. I wish to explain to you today that Christ Jesus, our Lord and our God, truly exists in your heart. The Kingdom of Heaven resides in your heart, dear children, and so do all its inhabitants! Christ is the Way, the Truth, and the Life as demonstrated by biblical teachings. Therefore, Christ is around you and through you, within you and outside you, before you and behind you, and above you and below you.

There is no place in the universe in which Christ does not exist. In the same breath, I hasten to tell you that there is also no place in your physical body in which Christ does not exist. The Energy of Christ is the whole of life that vibrates on Earth, in you and around you, in the air you breathe, in the water you drink, and in the Earth where you walk. Christ is everywhere, my beloveds. Christ is in you.

I love you.

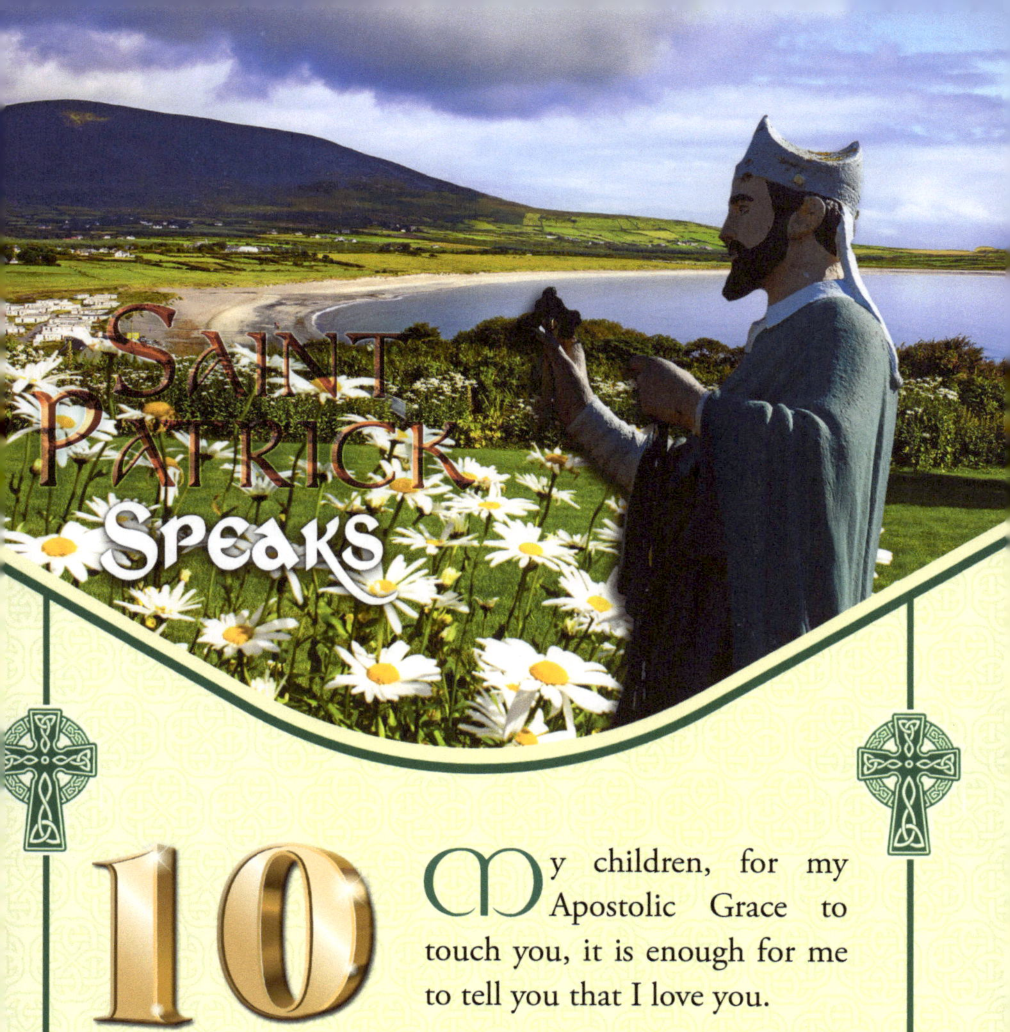

Saint Patrick Speaks

10

My children, for my Apostolic Grace to touch you, it is enough for me to tell you that I love you.

The wonderful miracle that allows me to speak to you today through this book, which has been blessed by God, is a gift from Heaven without equal on Earth. The work of Redemption of the five crosses accomplished to perfection by Saint Paul the Apostle paid the necessary price for the abolition of the obstacles that exist between your human soul and my Divine Soul.

On the Day of Judgment, the extraordinary value of having read my words here will be made clear to you.

~ Saint Patrick

Blessed be the Father for granting so much Mercy on your soul! Blessed be Marie-Josée, who takes this dictation from me today! Without Marie-Josée, my Sacred Words coming directly from Heaven would not have reached you. Listen very attentively to my Words, dear hearts, for the Redemption of your soul is found therein, in the Name of Christ the Savior and the Immaculate Heart of Mary. Christ is in you.

I love you.

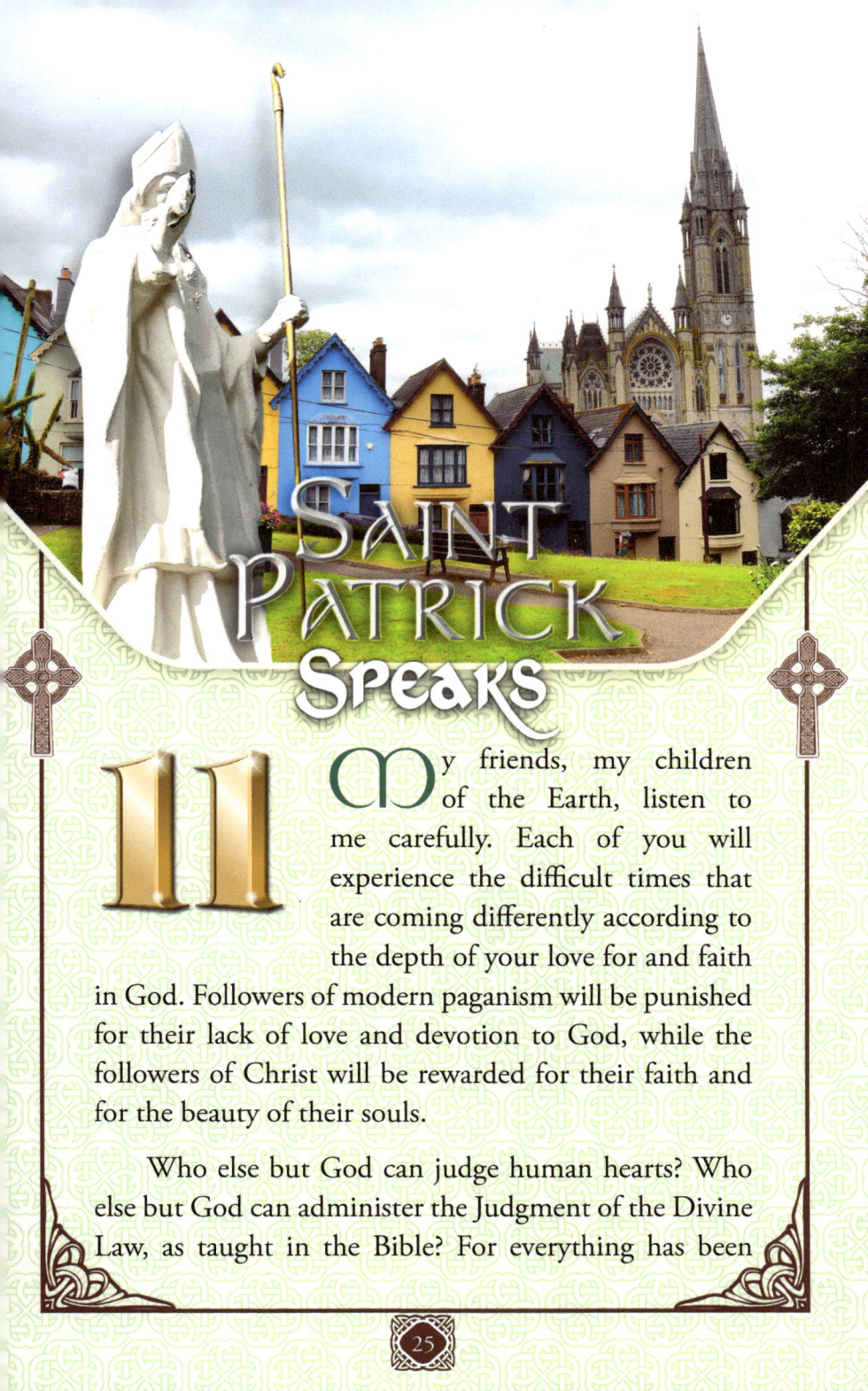

Saint Patrick Speaks

11

My friends, my children of the Earth, listen to me carefully. Each of you will experience the difficult times that are coming differently according to the depth of your love for and faith in God. Followers of modern paganism will be punished for their lack of love and devotion to God, while the followers of Christ will be rewarded for their faith and for the beauty of their souls.

Who else but God can judge human hearts? Who else but God can administer the Judgment of the Divine Law, as taught in the Bible? For everything has been explained by Jesus Christ our Savior to His Apostles, as is written in the New Testament. The Prophets and the events of the Old Testament foretold and prepared for the coming of Christ. Throughout the history of humanity, God's messengers have taken His Divine Word to the four corners of the Earth, as God asked me to do when I once walked the land of Ireland.

Everything is available for you to read, study, meditate, and share the Word of God through the Teaching of Christ who lives in you. Listen to Christ, who speaks inside of you, obey His commands, say yes to His Model of Perfection, and be courageous as Christ Himself was. The events to come will be a source of Liberation and internal Peace in spite of the planetary torments that will fall. Christ is in you. I love you.

Saint Patrick Speaks

12

My friends, dear friends of the Earth, listen to me carefully. Today, dear hearts, I desire to take you to Paradise with me. Since my physical death in 659, I inhabited Paradise among the Angels of God, the Saints in Paradise, the pure Souls, the Most Holy Virgin Mary, Christ Jesus our Savior and our God, the Holy Spirit, God the Father Almighty, as well as other Cosmic Forces unknown to you.

Here in Paradise, my friends, is the Perfect and Eternal Happiness of the Beatitudes of the Great Beyond, as promised by the Father. The Joy in our Divine Hearts is inexpressible, the Peace in our Minds is eternal and without comparison, and the Beauty of the landscapes in Paradise is of a magnificence that surpasses your wildest dreams. Life in Paradise is exquisite in all its aspects; our Happiness is real and without limit, and the pleasure of seeing and being with the Master Jesus cannot be expressed by words contained in the language of men.

Dear friends, dear hearts, Paradise will be given to you as well if you continue your study of the Bible and of the sacred texts approved by the Church and if you agree to believe in the authenticity of the Words you read and the Voice you hear, for faith in me, Saint Patrick, Apostle of Ireland, and faith in the other Saints in Paradise who speak to you through this collection of books blessed by God, will assure you of our perpetual help in opening the Doors of Paradise after the passage that is death. Say "Yes, Jesus, I love you." Say "Yes, Mary, I love you." Say "Yes, God the Father, I love you." Say "Yes, Holy Spirit, I love you." Say "Yes, Angels of the Father, I love you." Christ is in you.

I love you.

Saint Patrick Speaks

13

My friends, my children in the Grace of God, I love you. Listen to me well. Today, you will experience a day unlike any other. The enemy will not approach you, evil will not materialize, and the negativity of society will not touch you, for I will walk with you right next to Christ.

Know, dear hearts, that Christ Jesus, our Savior and our God, always walks with you, because He is in you—as are all the inhabitants of Paradise, including me. Christ is in you, dear friends, and He is with you from the moment of your birth until the moment of your death.

From today onward, realize in your heart that Christ Jesus, our Master and our Lord, and I, Saint Patrick, Apostle of Ireland, live in you and around you, breathe in you and around you, and walk with you and around you. This is why the enemy will not come near you. Christ is in you.

I love you.

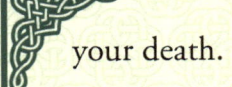

Saint Patrick Speaks

14

My children, my dearest children of the Earth, listen to me carefully. It is difficult to speak to you about Christ without awakening the fear of God's Judgment in you. Indeed, every moment of your life that has not been inspired by Christ, shared with Christ, and accomplished in the Name of Christ, will be judged by God the Father Almighty, for everything that is not of Christ is the enemy of Christ.

How, you will ask me, can we obtain God's Mercy when our life up to this point has been very pale in regards to the works of Christ through us? This is why you need the divine help of the Saints in Paradise to amend your life and repair the errors of the past. I will assist you in this. Christ is in you.

I love you.

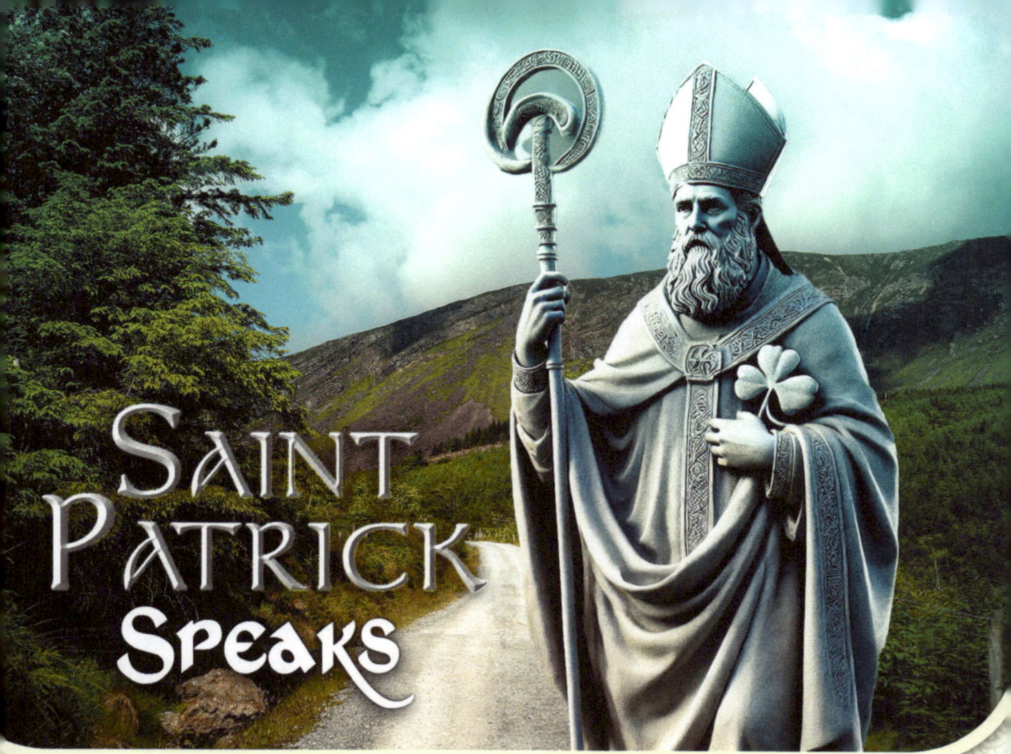

Saint Patrick Speaks

15

My friends, my children of the Earth, listen to me carefully. Today, I teach you of the virtues that please the Father, who rejoices in the souls who approach Him with humility and simplicity.

Remember that Jesus of Nazareth was humble and simple in every way. So, dear friends, approach Him in the same manner. Furthermore, the Father rejoices in the erudition of the Sacred Words contained in the Bible. Thus, take the time every day to read a few pages of the Bible and ask the Holy Spirit to enlighten you in your understanding of the Word of God.

Pray with me and frequently ask for my intercession.

~ Saint Patrick

The Father also rejoices in the rare pearl that is Love lived in the heart. I compare Love to a rare pearl, as, in fact, true and sincere Love is a Divine Gift that only Christ can offer to hearts that give themselves to Him. The Father rejoices in efforts and well-ordered work.

Indeed, the Father blesses tireless workers who waste no time and who make extraordinary efforts in order to accomplish their mission on Earth to perfection to himself.

Finally, the Father rejoices in hearts that pray, for prayer is the way par excellence of communication with Him. Be assured, dear children, that every prayer you utter is heard and received in the Heart of the Father, who is Love and Mercy. Christ is in you.

I love you.

Saint Patrick Speaks

16

My friends, my children of the Earth, listen to me well, as this is not to be taken lightly. I say unto you, I say unto you verily: the events to come will be atrocious. I hasten to tell you, in the same breath, that the assistance of Heaven during these difficult times will be extraordinary. This is why you must prepare yourselves now and increase the Vibrations of the Christ within you as much as possible, for Christ is indeed in you. I repeat it unto you!

Christ in you is the part of you that prays, that loves, that forgives, that abandons itself completely to the Father, and that is strong and upright. The Peace of Christ will remain within you despite the torments from outside. Our interactions with you from Heaven will be fluid and effective. The Mercy of God will be manifested within you frequently and in abundance. Christ is in you.

    I love you.

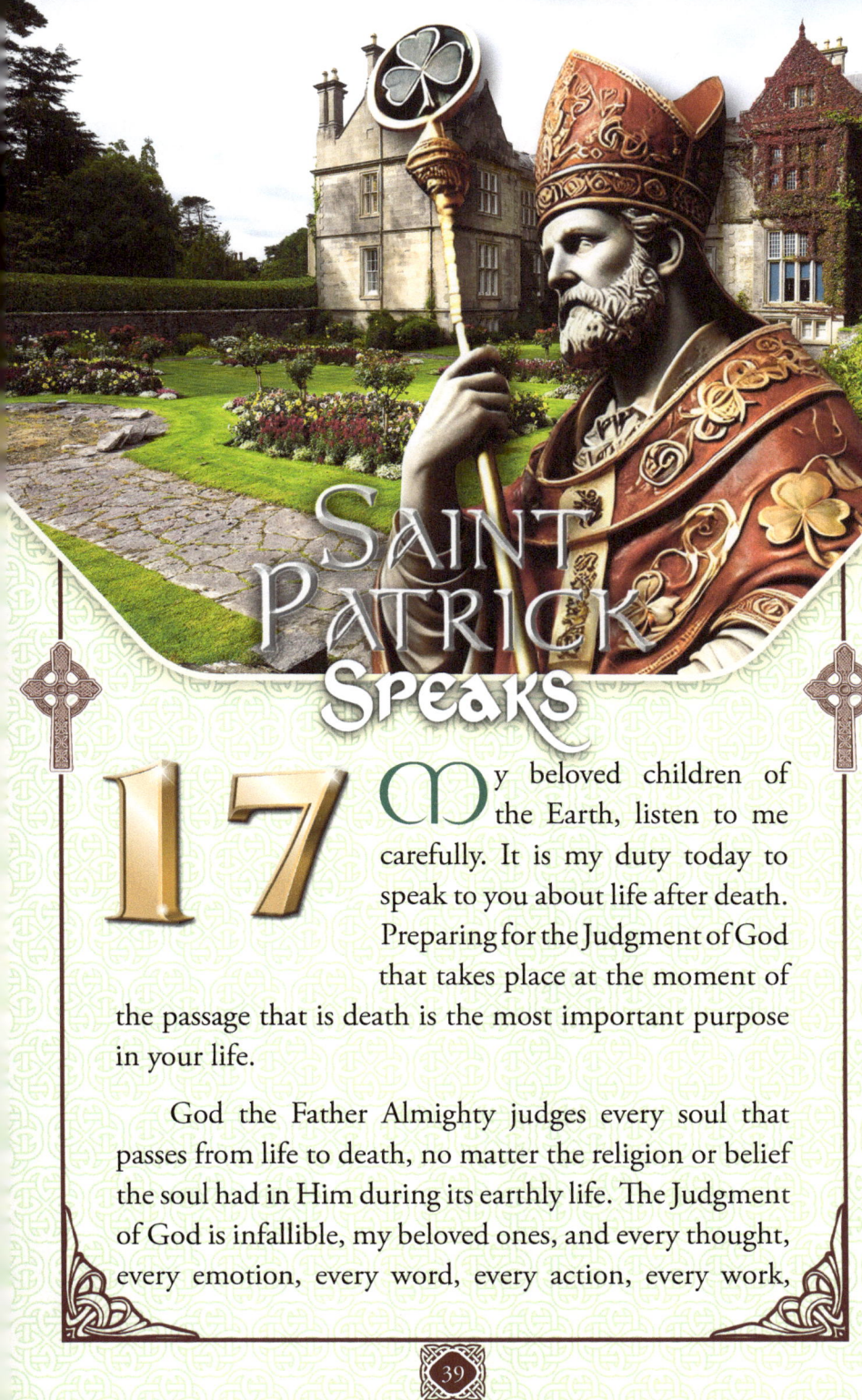

Saint Patrick Speaks

17

My beloved children of the Earth, listen to me carefully. It is my duty today to speak to you about life after death. Preparing for the Judgment of God that takes place at the moment of the passage that is death is the most important purpose in your life.

God the Father Almighty judges every soul that passes from life to death, no matter the religion or belief the soul had in Him during its earthly life. The Judgment of God is infallible, my beloved ones, and every thought, every emotion, every word, every action, every work, that has taken place during your life, second by second, will be judged. Are you ready?

You must prepare for death, my beloved ones, you must prepare to meet God today. I will assist you. Christ is in you.

I love you.

Saint Patrick Speaks

18

My dear friends, listen to me carefully. It is impossible for me to ignore the sad fate that is reserved for nonbelievers. The upcoming events will torment them on all levels. The pangs of purgatory and hell experienced after death are too intense and too horrible to be revealed here. My message today reminds you of your obligation to spread the Word of God to those around you.

Indeed, you are obliged to evangelize the souls who live around you—in fact, the souls that God has sent you—because this is written in the Bible. Not only will you feel a deep and lasting peace and joy throughout this process, but the Holy Spirit will place wise words and decisive arguments in your mouth in order to convert those around you. Above all, you will allow your loved ones to accompany you to Paradise immediately after the passage that is death. What a beautiful gift of Love to give to those we love! Christ is in you.

    I love you.

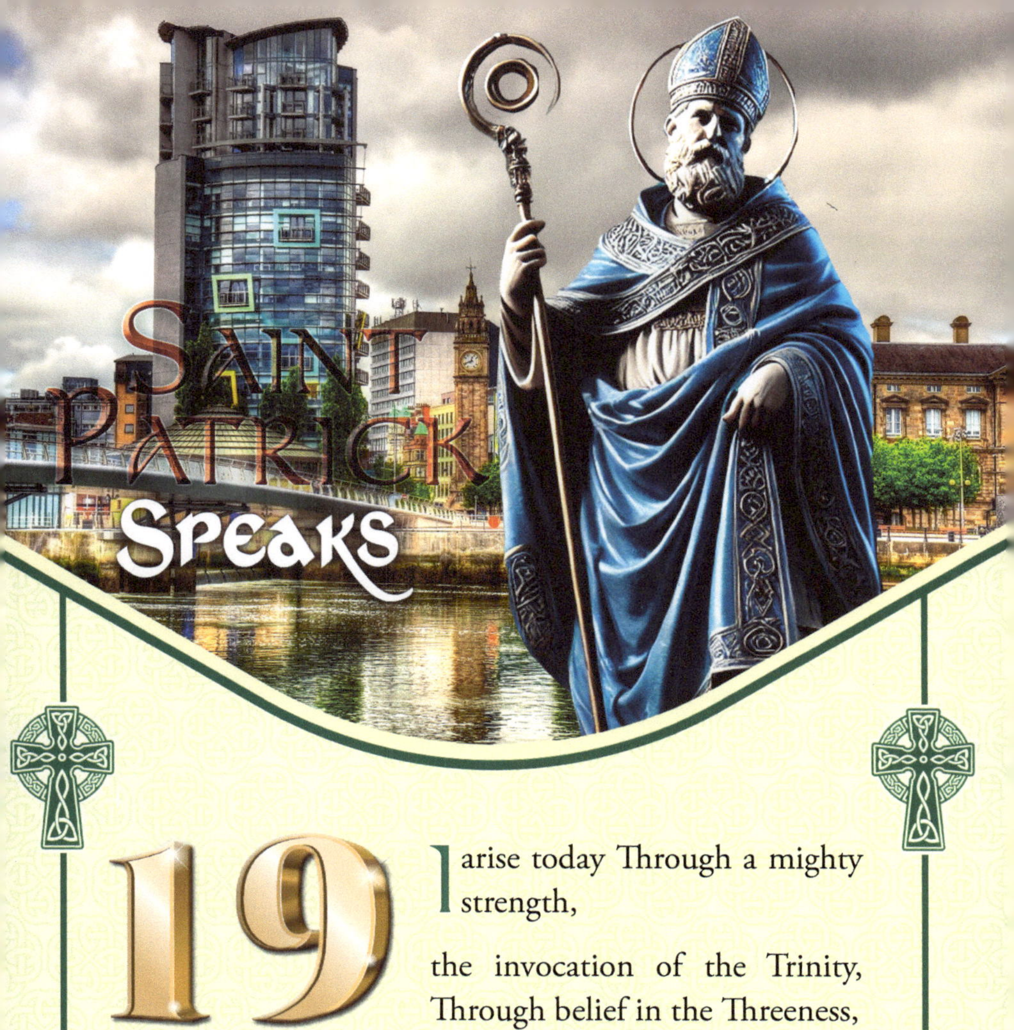

Saint Patrick Speaks

19

I arise today Through a mighty strength, the invocation of the Trinity, Through belief in the Threeness, Through confession of the Oneness of the Creator of creation.
I arise today Through the strength of Christ's birth with His baptism,
Through the strength of His crucifixion with His burial,
Through the strength of His resurrection with His ascension,
Through the strength of His descent for the judgment of doom.

I arise today Through the strength of the love of cherubim,
In the obedience of angels, In the service of archangels,
In the hope of resurrection to meet with reward, In the prayers of patriarchs, In the predictions of prophets,
In the preaching of apostles, In the faith of confessors,
In the innocence of holy virgins, In the deeds of righteous men.

I arise today,
through The strength of heaven,
The light of the sun,
The radiance of the moon,
The splendour of fire,
The speed of lightning,
The swiftness of wind,
The depth of the sea,
The stability of the earth,
The firmness of rock.

I arise today,
through God's strength to pilot me,
God's might to uphold me,
God's wisdom to guide me,
God's eye to look before me,
God's ear to hear me,
God's word to speak for me,
God's hand to guard me,

God's shield to protect me,
God's host to save me From snares of devils,
From temptation of vices,
From everyone who shall wish me ill, afar and near.

I summon today All these powers between me and those evils,
Against every cruel and merciless power that may oppose my body and soul,
Against incantations of false prophets, Against black laws of pagandom,
Against false laws of heretics,
Against craft of idolatry,
Against spells of witches and smiths and wizards,
Against every knowledge that corrupts man's body and soul;
Christ to shield me today Against poison,
against burning, Against drowning,
against wounding,
So that there may come to me an abundance of reward.

Christ with me,
Christ before me,
Christ behind me,
Christ in me,
Christ beneath me,
Christ above me,
Christ on my right,

Christ on my left,
Christ when I lie down,
Christ when I sit down,
Christ when I arise,
Christ in the heart of every man who thinks of me,
Christ in the mouth of everyone who speaks of me,
Christ in every eye that sees me,
Christ in every ear that hears me.

St. Patrick's Breastplate: Prayer For Protection

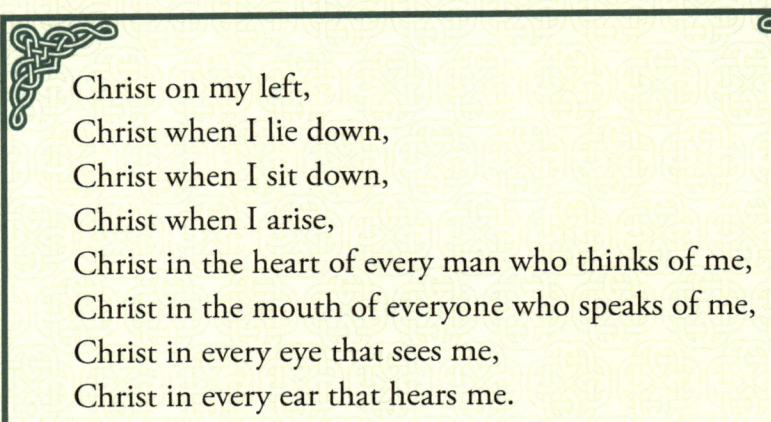

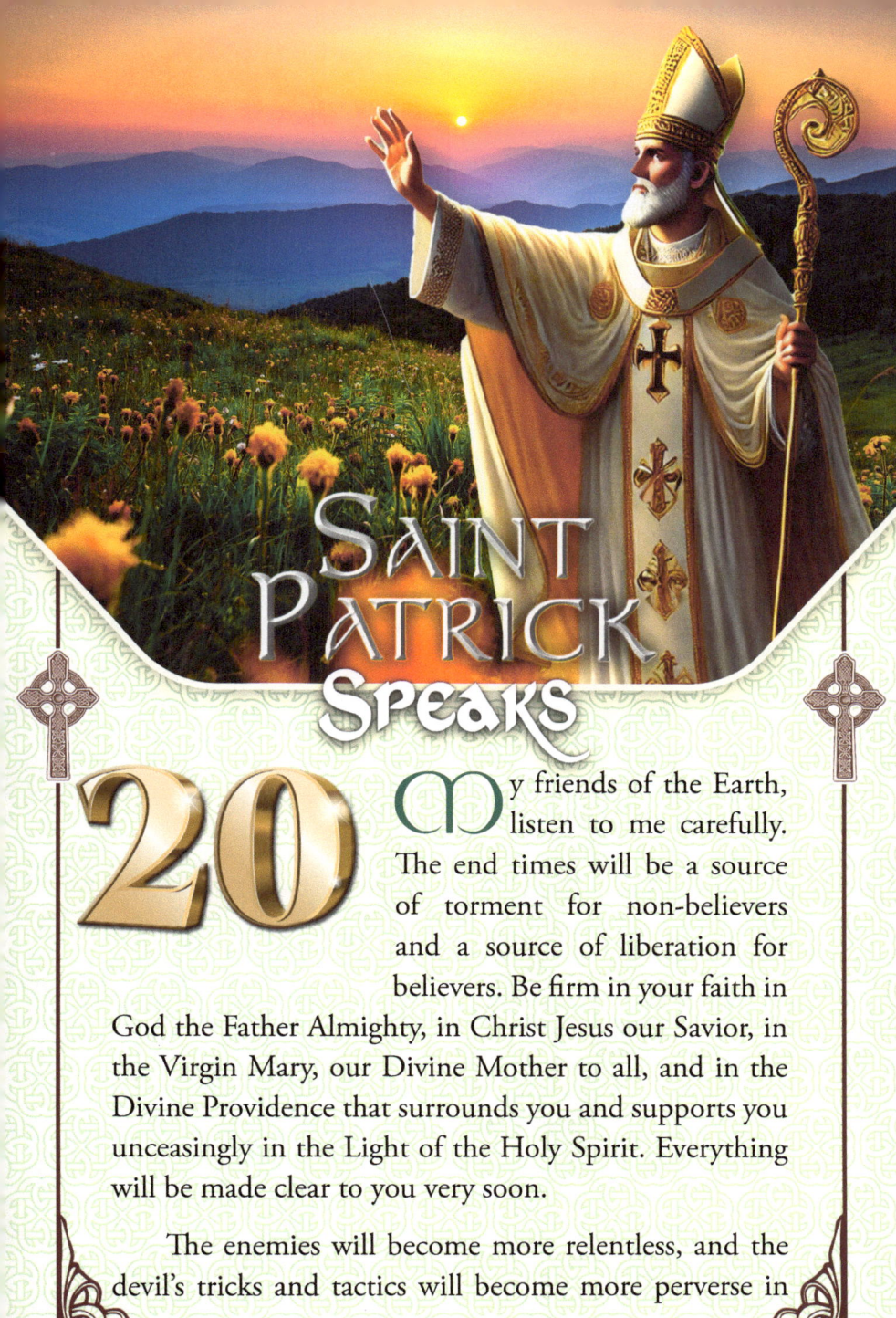

Saint Patrick Speaks

20

My friends of the Earth, listen to me carefully. The end times will be a source of torment for non-believers and a source of liberation for believers. Be firm in your faith in God the Father Almighty, in Christ Jesus our Savior, in the Virgin Mary, our Divine Mother to all, and in the Divine Providence that surrounds you and supports you unceasingly in the Light of the Holy Spirit. Everything will be made clear to you very soon.

The enemies will become more relentless, and the devil's tricks and tactics will become more perverse in

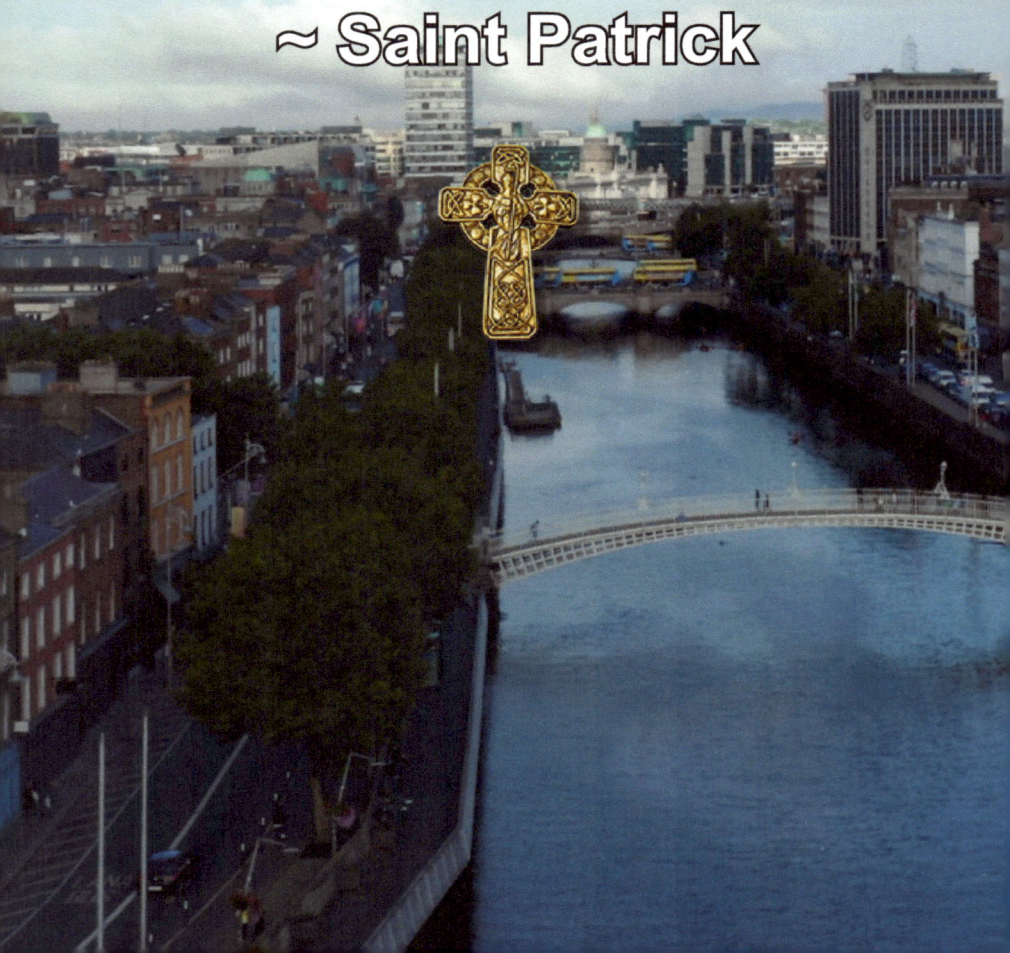

Say this often: "Saint Patrick of Ireland, guardian of the Catholic Spiritual Heritage, pray for us."

~ Saint Patrick

order to make you waver in your faith. Ignore all these false inner calls that speak to you of fear, anger, shame, and loneliness. The ego—that is, this collection of psychological errors that you carry within you and that are manipulated by the devil—soon will be completely eliminated by your prayers coupled with our Divine Assistance. Be firm and strong, I repeat it unto you, and the Miracles of abundance and consolation will be given to you by God Himself. Christ is in you.

I love you.

Saint Patrick Speaks

21

My friends on Earth, my dear sheep, listen to me carefully. Today, more than any other day in your life, do me the pleasure of returning to your childhood for a few minutes. Remember the dreams you had then, the purity of your intentions, the grandeur of your visions, and the immensity that was the rest of your life.

Today, my darling, make a mental comparison between the state of mind you had as a child and the state of mind you have now. What happened? Do you have many broken dreams, unexplored talents, wasted time, and paths that led nowhere? My friend, my beloved, you must ask God for forgiveness for tarnishing your soul with the defilements accumulated throughout your life. Everything that has taken place in your life that has taken place outside the Light of Christ is a sin that must be atoned for. Christ is in you.

I love you.

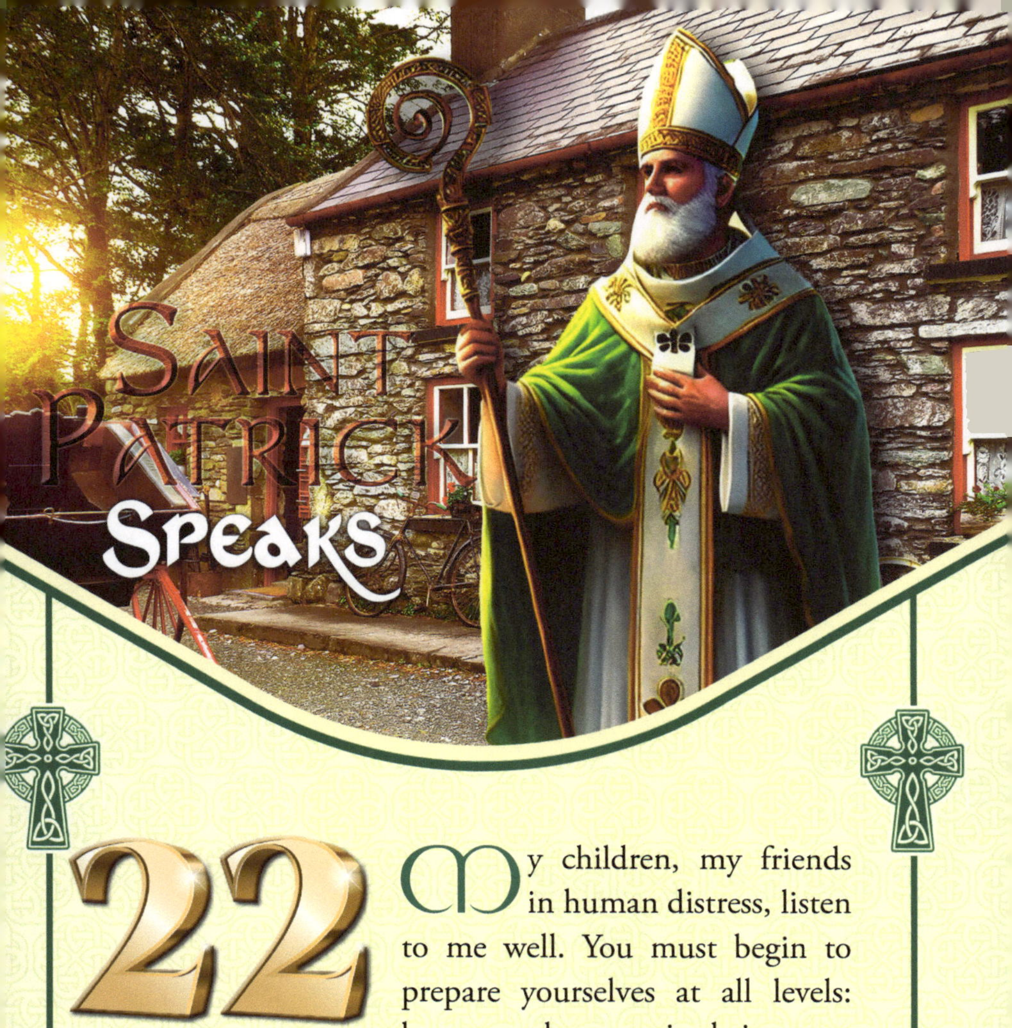

Saint Patrick Speaks

22

My children, my friends in human distress, listen to me well. You must begin to prepare yourselves at all levels: be properly organized in your residence with regard to water and survival supplies. Surround yourself with religious relics placed on all the walls around you.

Mentally prepare yourself to pray continuously no matter how serious the events in the world or immediately at your doors become. Become adequately and emotionally prepared to love and forgive, and do not judge those who would harm you, as you would be persecuted.

Be spiritually prepared to die if such is the Will of God; submit yourselves to the Sacrament of Confession regularly.

Continue your prayers with even greater fervor, urgency, and hope, and recite the rosary, the traditional prayers of the devoted Christian, and the basic prayers in Latin daily. The Father will be pleased in all this, and the Assistance of Heaven in its entirety will be given to you. Christ is in you.

I love you.

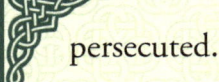

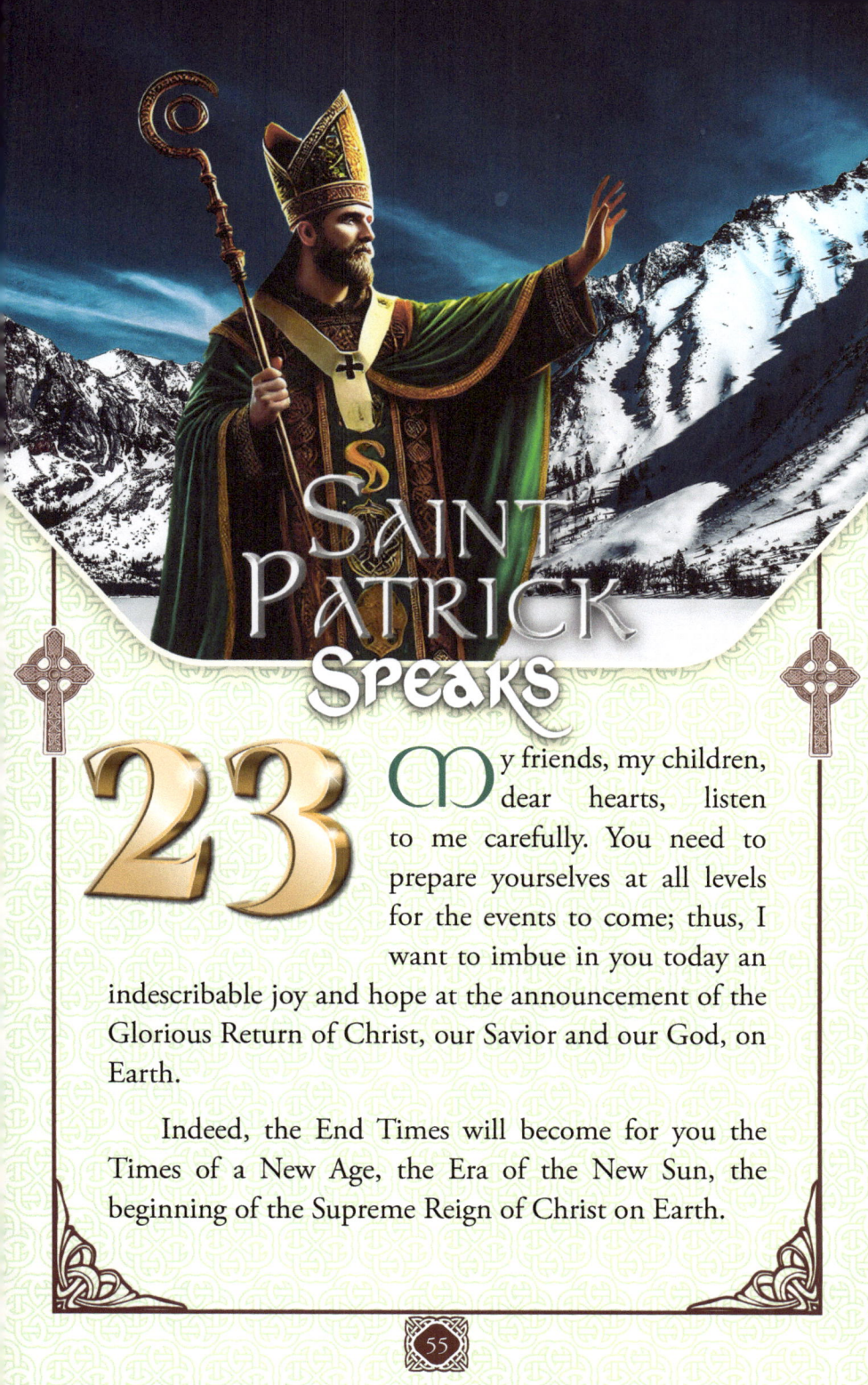

Saint Patrick Speaks

23

My friends, my children, dear hearts, listen to me carefully. You need to prepare yourselves at all levels for the events to come; thus, I want to imbue in you today an indescribable joy and hope at the announcement of the Glorious Return of Christ, our Savior and our God, on Earth.

Indeed, the End Times will become for you the Times of a New Age, the Era of the New Sun, the beginning of the Supreme Reign of Christ on Earth.

Evil will be completely eliminated on Earth; the darkness will be lifted, and suffering will disappear. Satan and his armies will be annihilated forever.

Amen! Alleluia! Be happy and have joy of the heart, for the End Times will have as their goal the Times of the Beginning and the birth of a new civilization based only on Christ. Christ is in you.

I love you.

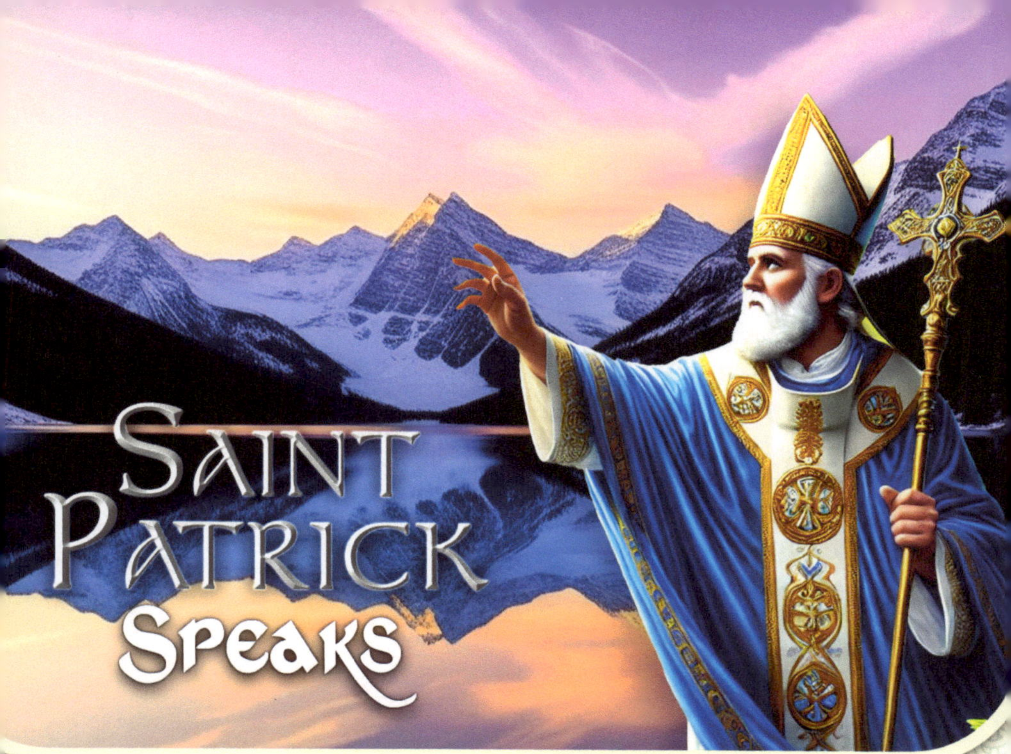

Saint Patrick Speaks

24

My children, my friends, listen to me carefully. It is clear that from today on, the rest of your life will be completely different. By this, I imply that profound changes will occur in your external and internal living environments. Indeed, new elements in your life will arise at all levels, including changes in your employment, place of residence, circle of friends, and the activities you enjoy during your free time. You will feel drawn to everything that surrounds the Life of Christ: His History, His Power today in your heart, His Influence on the present Church, and the future that He offers you.

You will be more inclined to read the Bible, to go to Mass, and to participate in the Sacrament of the Eucharist as well as to submit yourself to the Holy Sacrament of Confession. This is very good. Know that through all these moments of transition, the Father draws closer to you and that He carries you in His Heart and brings you ever closer to Him. Christ is in you.

I love you.

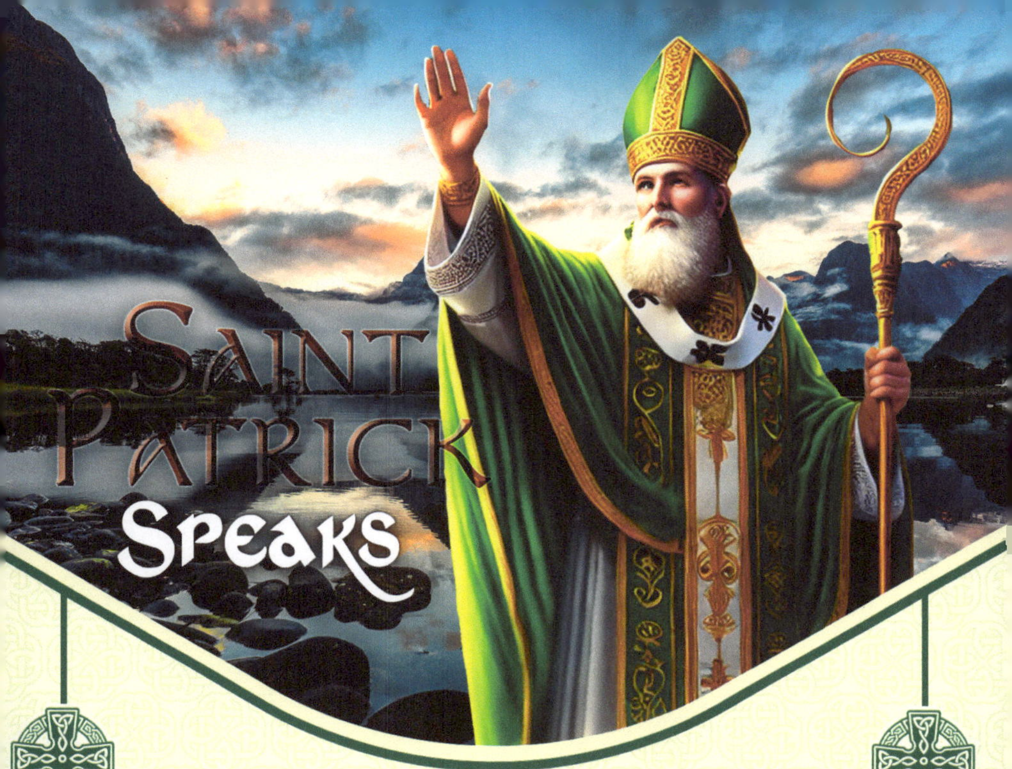

Saint Patrick Speaks

25

My friends, my children, listen to me carefully. The life that was given to you at birth—in fact, at the moment of conception, in fact—does not belong to you, nor to your parents, nor to the cells that form your physical body, nor to nature in general. The life given to you is the Life of Christ and is One with the Holy Trinity. Christ, who became flesh under the Holy Name of Jesus of Nazareth 2,000 years ago, is the very Foundation of all life on Earth and who animates all the creatures created by God the Father.

For the Father, the Son, and the Holy Spirit are One, One Holy Trinity, Universal and Eternal, for ever and ever, world without end. I bless you in the Name of the Father, and of the Son, and of the Holy Spirit. Amen. Christ is in you.

I love you.

Saint Patrick Speaks

26

My friends, my children, listen to me carefully.

Today, I would like to tell you how much I love you! My Love goes far beyond Ireland and has remained in me even after my death. It embraces all nations, all hearts, and all souls that seek God! My human love has transformed into Divine Love here in Paradise, and this Love envelops you, guides you, and protects you, here, now, and forever! Let us give thanks to God for granting so much Mercy on your soul. Christ is in you. I love you.

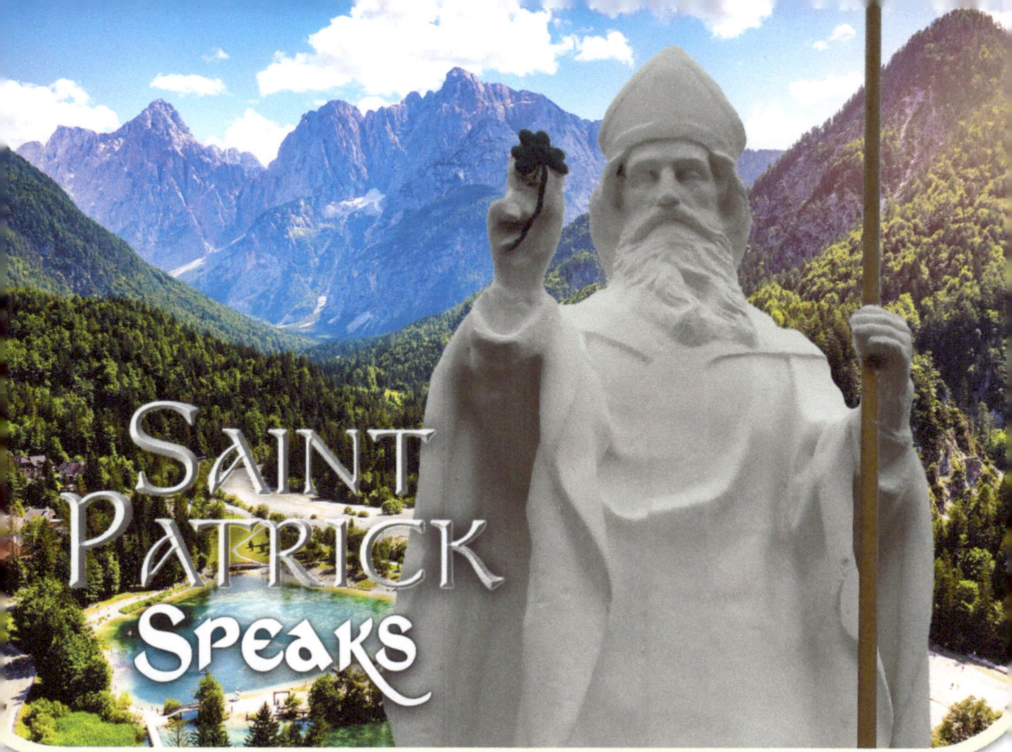

Saint Patrick Speaks

27

My friends, my children, do not listen to the rumors around you about the end of the world. The Father is preparing for the Great Day of Judgment; this is true. It is true that the whole Earth will undergo atrocious and extreme changes. I say unto you, I say unto you verily: the Day of the Great Judgment of God is at your doorstep.

However, only God alone knows the exact moment of the beginning of the purifying events to come. I have already told you, and I repeat the same unto you: Do not trust the rumors that are circulating around the Earth about the end of the world as well as the fictitious dates that are presented to you, for God alone decides everything, absolutely everything; He decides what takes place on Earth—both the small events and the big events—and the precise date and time of His Judgment belongs exclusively to Him. Christ is in you.

I love you.

AFTERWORD

Saint Patrick and I are holding your hands as you read these lines. We await you at the Gates of Paradise after the passage that is death.

I bless you, and I love you.

Saint John Paul II

Marie-Josée Thibault's life is in no way similar to yours. When she wakes, the saints of Heaven visit her, talk to her, teach her, and pray intensely with her. When such mystical sessions draw to a close, she greets with great respect and deep reverence the Masters of the Heavenly Court. This servant of the Lord spends the rest of the day in the company of her guardian angel, who continues her spiritual education and ceaselessly protects her from the perils of this fallen world.

Bestowed by the Heavenly Father, her gifts of clairvoyance and clairaudience allow her to remain in continuous contact with the supernatural dimension juxtaposed with ours, where the soul is born of the Spirit through Jesus and Mary. She prays that, one day soon, the entire human race will give glory to the Father, the Son, and the Holy Spirit.

ABOUT THE AUTHOR

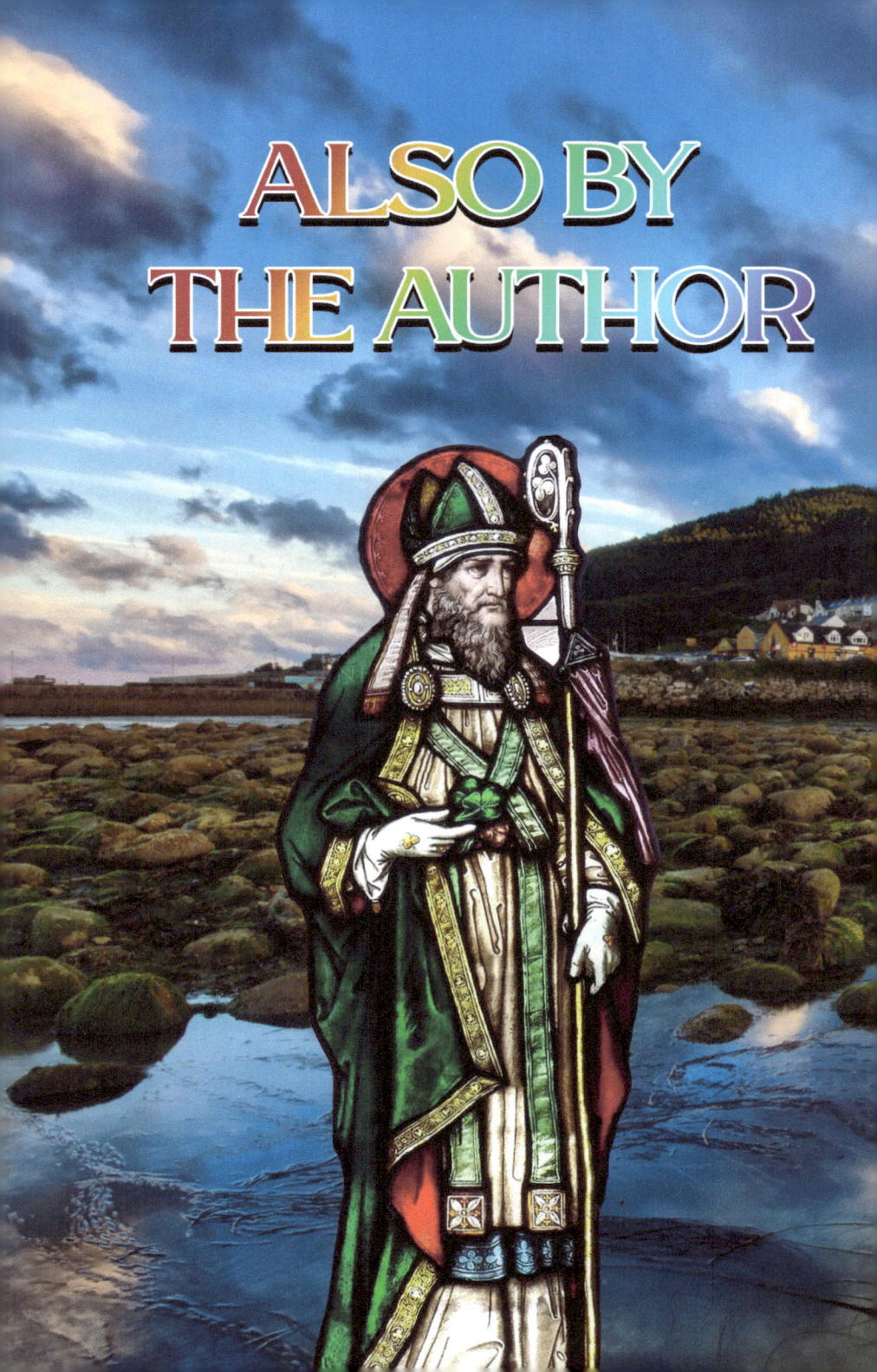

ALSO BY THE AUTHOR

- Abba, Your Father, Speaks: Book I
- Abba, Your Father, Speaks: Book II
- Abba, Your Father, Speaks: Book III
- Abba, Your Father, Speaks: Book IV
- Dear Humanity: Book 1
- Dear Humanity: Book 2
- Dear Humanity: Book 3
- St Therese of Lisieux Speaks - Book 1: I Am The Heart of the Rose
- Saint Francis of Assisi Speaks - Book 1
- Saint Francis of Assisi Speaks - Book 2
- Saint Martin de Porres Spaeaks - Book 1
- Saint Bernadette Speaks - Book 1
- Saint Joan of Arc Speaks - Book 1
- Saint Padre Pio Speaks: Book 1
- Saint Padre Pio Speaks: Book 2
- Saint Padre Pio Speaks: Book 3
- Saint Beethoven Speaks - Book 1
- Saint Barnabas Speaks - Book 1
- Angel Gabriel Speaks: Book 1
- The Holy Pope Saint John Paul II Speaks - Book 1
- The Holy Pope Saint John Paul II Speaks - Book 2
- Prophet Moses Speaks 1
- Saint John the Baptist Speaks

www.ingramcontent.com/pod-product-compliance
Lightning Source LLC
Chambersburg PA
CBHW040456240426
43663CB00033B/28